What Jewish People Believe

A Look at Judaism

Jeffrey D. Johnson

Wipf & Stock
PUBLISHERS
Eugene, Oregon

Wipf and Stock Publishers
199 W 8th Ave, Suite 3
Eugene, OR 97401

What Jewish People Believe
A Look at Judaism
By Johnson, Jeffrey D.

ISBN 13: 978-1-55635-081-8
ISBN 10: 1-55635-081-3
Publication date 11/30/2006

About Israel Today Ministries

Three-fold Purpose:

- Teach the Church about Israel
- Teach Israel about their Messiah
- Help feed those in need (Romans 15:27; Genesis 12:1-3)

To receive Dr. Johnson's "teaching letters," or, if you would like to send a gift to Israel Today Ministries, or if you would like Dr. Johnson to speak at your church event, school, or small group, contact:

Israel Today Ministries
P.O. Box 150288
Arlington, TX 76015
Phone/Fax 817.468.4441
E mail: Galileeman@juno.com

This is Yossef (Joseph) and Abigail. Your monthly donations help feed little ones like these.

"Inasmuch as ye have done it unto one of the least of these my brethren, ye have done it unto me" –Jesus, Matthew 25:40

About Dr. Jeffrey D. Johnson

- Three decades in ministry
- Founder/Director of Israel Today Ministries
- Director of tours to the Middle East
- Senior pastor in Ohio, Massachusetts and California
- Almost 7 years directorship with International Ministries to Israel (formerly, The American Association for Jewish Evangelism, where the famed Hyman Appelman was the first president)
- Conference speaker
- Bible expositor
- Guest lecturer
- Author

Born and raised in the Midwest, Dr. Johnson took his B.D. from Massillon Baptist College, his MA from Moody Bible Institute, and his Th.M. and Th.D. from Christian Bible College. His passion for Israel, the Jewish roots of Christianity and Bible prophecy, is well known. His teaching will stir your heart to follow the Lord and to love and *"pray for the peace of Jerusalem"* (Psalm 122:6).

As an "Itinerant Bible Teacher," Dr. Johnson will travel anywhere to proclaim God's redeeming Grace through our Lord and Savior Jesus the Messiah, *"to the Jew first, and also to the Greek"* (Romans 1:16).

His call is to *"Teach the Church about Israel; Teach Israel about their Messiah; and to feed those in need"* (Genesis 12:3; Romans 15:27).

Dr. Jeff and his wife, Louise, have purposed to serve the Lord trusting God to provide the funds and resources for their livelihood.

Israel Today Ministries, founded by Dr. Johnson, is a faith ministry, supported by "love offerings" from those desiring to bless Israel. Dr. Jeff and Louise have been commissioned and sent out by their home church.

Comments from Christian Leaders

I am pleased to recommend him to churches as an able expositor of the Word of God.

– *the late* **John Walvoord**, Chancellor,
Dallas Theological Seminary

A Bible Expositor with special insights on the origin, nature and destiny of God's chosen people, Israel.

– **John C. Whitcomb**, Bible Scholar, Author, Professor

A careful expositor of Scripture.

– **Homer Kent**, President Emeritus,
Grace College and Seminary

A practitioner of all that he preaches.

– **Paige Patterson**, former President of the
Southern Baptist Convention, President,
Southeastern Baptist Theological Seminary

He has a wonderful grasp of Jewish history and liturgy.

– **Edgar C. James**, Professor, Moody Bible Institute

He is a person who has been uniquely prepared by God to preach and teach about God's special people. Any one who hears him will come away with a great love for the people of Abraham.

–**Dick Dahlquist**, Chair, Pastoral Studies, Acting Dean,
Grace College of Graduate Studies

He has a gifted teaching ministry which encompasses Biblical prophecy and insights into modern-day Judaism.

–the late **Paul Tassell**, Bible Scholar, Author,
former National Representative of the G.A.R.B.C.

He has a great ministry.

– **LaVerne Butler**, former President of Mid-Continent Baptist College, Scholar, Conference Speaker, President, Pulpit Aflame

Your heart will be thrilled as he ministers the prophetic Scriptures.

– the late **Alden A. Gannett**, President Emeritus of Southeastern Bible College, Bible Scholar, Author, Conference Speaker, President, Gannett Ministries

He loves the people and nation of Israel. He has given himself to a thorough study of God's ancient people and of the prophetic.

– **Ivan H. French**, Pastor Emeritus, Pleasant View Bible Church, former Professor, Grace College and Seminary

Table of Contents

Chapter 1
What Jewish People Believe

Four Main Divisions of Judaism:

1. *Orthodox*
   Orthodox Judaism believes in a personal Messiah, who though not divine, is super-human. They also embrace the authority of the Scriptures in conjunction with tradition.

2. *Conservative*
   Conservative Judaism is, philosophically, the middle of the road Judaism. They believe that tradition is not fixed, but rather is changeable. Conservative Jews are not strict in the traditions and expectations as are the Orthodox.

3. *Reform*
   Reform Judaism is the liberal branch of Judaism and is diametrically opposite to the tradition and trappings of Orthodox Judaism. They embrace an all-inclusive stance to religion and tradition.

4. *Reconstructionism*
   Reconstructionism is a branch that was founded in the early 1900's by Rabbi Mordecai Kaplan. Reconstructionists believe that Judaism is not just a religion, but a civilization, a totality of lifestyle. This includes language, art, philosophy, folklore, tradition and science.

   *(There are also other sub-groups that fall within the construct of these four main divisions, such as Humanistic Judaism and Chasidic Judaism).

L'Chaim - To Life

L'chaim is a Hebrew word used in the celebration of Jewish life extensively. From birth to the grave there is a celebration of existence B cherishing children, mom, dad, and grandparents. These celebrations have a great range from teenagers experiencing Bar/Bat Mitzvah, a rite of passage into adulthood and becoming a member of the religious community, to the marriage ceremony that remind Jewish families that the temple in Jerusalem is destroyed and anticipates redemption through the Messiah or the messianic age to come. Lighting candles to remember loved ones who have passed on is another of the many ways a Jew celebrates life. Jews also encourage the freedom to mourn without restraint or fear of embarrassment. One main key to understanding Judaism is the understanding of how they celebrate life.

Theological Beliefs

The Bible

The Orthodox Jew believes that the Old Testament (Tenach) is inspired by God and is absolutely trustworthy. That God spoke to the prophets and writers of the Old Testament by divine inspiration as they were moved to write the exact words of God.

In contrast, the Reform (liberal) Jew believes that the Scriptures were not inspired by God alone. That the prophets and other writers were inspired like any other writer of literature is inspired, and that the authors embellished the story and used parables rather than exact words from God.

God

"I believe with a perfect faith that the Creator (blessed be His name) is one God, and that there is no unity whatever like unto Him; and that He alone is our God, who was, is and will be eternally." BMaimonidies, Thirteen Articles of Faith, Number 2

All Jews believe in this statement to one degree or another. Maimonidies (Jewish philosopher/physician, 1135-1204 A.D.) wrote what would be an equivalent to the Christian's "Apostle's Creed".

The Hebrew word translated "one" is usually the Hebrew word *"yachid"* which coveys the idea of "an absolute one". God instructed Abraham to take his "only"(*yachid*) son (Genesis 22:2). Whereas, in Deuteronomy 6:4 we find another word translated "one", the Hebrew word, *"Echod"*. "Hear, O

Israel: the Lord our God is one (*echod*) Lord." In Genesis 2:24 we read, "And they" (Adam and Eve) shall be "one flesh (*basar echod*). The idea of *"echod"* is diversity within unity, or that of a composite unity. Simply stated, a plurality within a single entity, such as a triune being, the Trinity.

Judaism does not embrace the Christian belief of the Trinity of the God-head (Father, Son, Holy Spirit), rather they believe that God is a single entity, God only. When a Jew, who embraces Judaism, states that he, believes in God, it is not the same as the Christian view.

Man

When it comes to the definition of man Judaism and Christianity are in agreement in some areas and poles apart in other. Christians believe that man, though created in the image of God, has fallen into sin because of Adam and therefore needs salvation by the grace of God through the shed blood of Jesus, "our Passover" lamb (Romans 5:12-21; 1 Corinthians 5:7) .

Judaism teaches that man, created in the image of God, is intrinsically good, and given the right surroundings and circumstances will make the right decisions. Also, that man can overcome evil through good and can retrace their steps and correct any wrongs that have been done. Judaism does not embrace the Christian doctrine of "original sin". Judaism believes that man has a spark of divine light within and can be all that God wants him/her to be by their own works or merit. However Christianity teaches that all have sinned and need redemption (Romans 3:10,23).

Sin

Judaism teaches that evil or sin is something that is contrary to principles taught within the Scripture. Sin is emphasized between man and God and that man can overcome sin through the study of Torah, good works and blessing others. Simply, by shear will power. Judaism does not believe in original sin or the sinful nature of man, therefore cannot explain why there is sin and evil in the world.

Salvation

When looking at the view of salvation held by the teaching of Judaism, one finds that it is quite different from that of Christianity. The Old Testament refers to salvation in terms of "atonement". The Day of Atonement (Yom Kippur) was the time when the High Priest offered a sacrifice for his sins and the sins of the nation Israel. Atonement was accomplished in this way. Atonement (Hebrew Kippur) means to cover. In the Old Testament sins were temporarily covered through sacrificial offerings, *"in the forbearance of God He passed over the sins previously committed"* (Romans 3:25) NASB.

In the Old Testament, God was acting in a just and holy fashion in temporality covering or "passing over" sins in anticipation of the coming of His Son as a sacrificed Lamb who would "take away" the sin, and not simply cover, or pass over sin. (John 1:29)

The only place these sacrifices could take place was in the Temple located in Jerusalem. Since the Temple is no longer standing a problem arose regarding what to do about the sacrifices and atonement for sin. The rabbinical leaders, subsequently, developed a new concept since the Temple was gone, and therefore, impossible to have blood sacrifice. They concluded that atonement may be accomplished by good deeds, prayer and repentance. That fulfilling these commandments was equivalent to the blood sacrifice of biblical times. Thus, Judaism developed an atonement or salvation through good works.

The Afterlife

The afterlife is an ambiguous concept for Judaism. They emphasize that Individuals live on through progeny, memory, personal influence in the world and, yes, the immortality of the soul. However, the location where the soul continues is not very clear. At best it is a fuller experience with God or divine bliss or eternal nothingness. The rabbis have very little to say in this area and can bring little comfort.

This is an area in which Christians can bring hope to their Jewish friends. In the Lord Jesus (Yeshua B Jewish way to say Jesus) Christians have the assurance in spending eternity with God in Heaven.

Heaven/Hell

The concept of heaven and hell according to Judaism is a way to reward the good and to equalize the evil in the universe.

Heaven is the place where the soul enters an experience with God and the Heavenly host. It is like the Garden of

Eden full of bliss and peace. It is a place where one can study Torah without restraint and with total freedom.

Hell is a place of burning and torment for the wicked. It is complete separation from God and the eternal bliss of Eden. Liberal Judaism rejects a literal place of heaven or hell. They would completely dismiss the reality of eternal existence in a geographical locale. Rather, they say it is metaphor and yet does not attempt to explain where the soul goes after death.

Messiah

Orthodox and Conservative Jews believe in a personal messiah, a super-human messiah, however, not a "God-Man" messiah. Judaism finds it difficult to justify a messiah being fully God and fully man at the same time. They believe this "super-human" , though not divine, messiah will bring about world peace and prosperity. Prayer is offered up each day for messianic redemption and restoration.

Liberal or reform Jews do not believe in a personal messiah, rather they look for a messianic age of peace, where the world will be one. They believe that man will bring about world peace and harmony.

Jesus

Most Jewish people believe that Jesus was a historical person, and a good Jew. However, they believe he was human like any other man and the son of God only in the context that all people are children, or sons of God. They believe that Jesus was great because of his teachings, lifestyle and impact on the world. But, they do not believe that He was God.

Chapter 2
Jewish Holy Days

The Jewish calendar is replete with celebration and reflection. Following are a few highlights regarding some of the Holy Days.

Rosh Hashanah: (September/October)

Rosh Hashanah begins the celebration of the Jewish New Year and is also a celebration of the creation of the universe. The shofar (ram's horn) is blown, special prayers are recited and the culmination of these events fall upon the holiest day in the Jewish year, Yom Kippur.

Yom Kippur: (September/October)

Yom Kippur or the Day of Atonement (Levitcus 23) begins 10 days after Rosh Hashanah, and is a time of prayer and fasting asking forgiveness for sins of the community as well as the individual. This is a time where, it is said that, God will judge the people of the earth and determine if they are to live throughout the next year or appoint their time to die. Thus, there is an emphasis on reading scripture, prayer, fasting and repentance. Rosh Hashanah and Yom Kippur are referred to as the "High Holy Days".

Sukkot: (September/October)

Sukkot, or the Feast of Tabernacles is a harvest festival of thanksgiving (Leviticus 23). In fact the pilgrims, in the beginning of American history, used the festival of Sukkot for their time of praise and thanksgiving, thus our holiday of Thanksgiving. This is a time of gathering the harvest and a time of remembering the wandering Israelites in the wilderness for forty years living in temporary dwellings or booths (a sukkah).

Simchat Torah: (October)

Simchat Torah, or Rejoicing in the Law celebrates the conclusion of weekly readings through the Torah (five books of Moses) in the Synagogue. They conclude by reading the last chapters of Deuteronomy and the beginning of Genesis. There is a great celebration parading the Torah Scroll up and down the isles of the Synagogue, dancing, singing and rejoicing.

Chanukah: (December)

Chanukah, or the Feast of Lights is an eight-day celebration remembering God's deliverance from the notorious Syrian emperor Antiochus who set out to destroy the Jewish religion. An eight candle menorah is lit, one candle the first night, two candles the second and so on. This is used to commemorate the victory of Mattathias and his five sons, including Judah the Maccabee ("Judah, the Hammer") who led a revolt against the Syrian emperor. When they defeated Antiochus, who desecrated the Temple, they cleansed the Temple. The Jews endeavored to light the seven-candle Menorah located inside the Temple. However, there was only enough consecrated oil to last for one day. The miracle was that the Temple Menorah stayed lit for eight days until the special oil was procured. Thus the lighting of the eight candles is for the remembrance of this great event. Gifts are exchanged and special foods are eaten. It is a time of great celebration.

Purim: (February/March)

Purim or the Festival of Lots is a time of celebrating the redemption of the Jews from being exterminated. Because the Jews refused to bow down to Haman, a notorious Persian, he , being an advisor to King Ahasuerus, drew lots (Hebrew, *Purim*) to determine what day the Jews were to be killed. Through the efforts and intervention of Mordecai and his niece, Queen Esther, the Israelites were saved.

It is a time of celebration with costumes of the biblical characters. The Book of Esther is read in the synagogue and festive foods and noisemakers are part of the celebration.

Passover: (March/April)

Passover is celebrated in the Spring time. The celebration remembers the exodus of the Jews from Egypt. Special foods are prepared with each item symbolizing the biblical event. A special place is set for the prophet Elijah as they believe he will come during Passover and announce the coming of the Messiah.

Shavuot: (May/June)

Shavuot, or Feast of Pentecost occurs seven weeks after the second day of Passover and commemorates the receiving of the Law (Torah) at Mount Sinai. Passover, Shavuot and Sukkot are the three pilgrimage festivals. During the time of the Temple the Jews brought an offering of their firstfruits (*bikkurim*) to the Lord. Shavuot is also called the spring harvest Festival of firstfruits. Shavuot is considered the birthday of Judaism.

Shabbat: (begins Friday night – ends Saturday night)

Shabbat is considered the holiest day of the week. It is a time of celebrating the creation of the world. It is a day of rest, prayer, study, relaxation, romance, spirituality, enjoyment and setting aside this day from the rest of the week. God rested on this day (Gen. 2:3) and it is the only holy day mentioned in the Ten Commandments (Exodus 20:8).

There are many other wonderful holidays and celebrations throughout the Jewish year. These few examples will give Christians a general idea of what is celebrated, and why.

The Christian Connection

There are many parallels to the Christian calendar and the Jewish calendar. Below are theological connections that you may find surprising.

1. *Rosh HaShanah* is symbolic of the Rapture of the Church and the complete gathering of Israel (1 Cor. 15:52; Isa. 27:12-13).

2. *Yom Kippur* represents Israel's time of "Great Trouble" or the Tribulation Period (Zech. 12:10-13:1; Jer. 30:7: Heb. 9-10)

3. *Sukkot* points to the Millennium Reign of Messiah on earth (Rev. 21:3; Zech. 14).

4. *Simchat Torah* symbolizes believers rejoicing in the "Living Word" (John 1). Jesus the Messiah fulfilled the Law and is the Word.

5. *Chanukah* is mentioned in John 10 when Jesus was in Jerusalem during the "Feast of Dedication" or Chanukah. In that context Jesus said, "I am the good shepherd: the good shepherd giveth his life for the sheep" (10:11). In the lighting of the eight candles during Chanukah a ninth candle is used. This candle is raised above the other eight. This is called the *"shammash"* meaning "servant

or shepherd" candle. Jesus was saying, *"I am the good shammash"*

6. *Purim* is a reminder that God has a plan for redemption for Israel as well as the whole world. Jesus is our redeemer, protector and friend.

7. *Passover* points us to the Messiah who became our Passover (1 Cor. 5:7). Just as blood had to be spilled, and put around the doors in order for those who believed to be saved, so it is with Messiah Jesus. His blood had to be spilled in order for those who believe to be saved. Communion comes from the Passover tradition. The Bread and Wine come from the tradition. The Passover and the Lord's Supper tell of the complete story of redemption and deliverance. Jesus said that Elijah has already come. He was speaking of John the Baptist (Matthew17:12,13). Therefore, when Jewish people celebrate the Passover they unconsciously bear witness to the Messiah. When a Christian partakes of communion, they remember Jesus, of whom the Passover Lamb represented.

8. *Shavuot* remembers the receiving of the Law from Sinai. However, it also commemorates the receiving of the Holy Spirit on the Day of Pentecost (Shavuot) in Acts chapter two. Shavuot not only celebrates the birthday of Judaism, it is also the birthday of the Church.

9. *Shabbat* points to the true rest we find in the Messiah and ultimately the Sabbath rest of the Kingdom of Messiah (*Thy Kingdom Come*). Jesus said, *"Come to Me, all who are weary and heavy-laden, and I will give you rest" (Mat. 11:28).*

Believer's Responsibility

These holidays are shadows and types of Messiah. Most Jewish people are unaware of the meaning behind these beautiful Holy Days. Believers in Jesus have the responsibility and privilege to share their faith with Jewish people as to the meaning of these great symbols and types that are associated with Jewish celebration.

May God bless you as you bless God's ancient people Israel!

"So then faith cometh by hearing, and hearing by the world of God." Romans 10:17

Chapter 3
High Holy Days

Festive lights, special foods, games, family celebration, prayer, religious activity. What is going on within the Jewish community? Why are Jewish people praying and rejoicing?

During the months of September and October you will find your Jewish neighbors getting ready for the most important events of the Jewish calendar, the "High Holy Days".

In fact, the autumn and winter months are replete with the celebration of various Jewish holidays. Let's take a brief look at two of these wonderful moments of festivity, reflection, awe and self- examination.

Rosh Hashanah

Rosh Hashanah is the celebration of the Jewish civil New Year. Rosh, means "head" or "beginning", or the "start of" the New Year. This is a time when Jews celebrate the anniversary of the Creation of the world, universe and man (Genesis 1,2). [The Jewish sacred New Year begins at

Passover in the springtime]. Rosh Hashanah is a time of rejoicing and celebration as well as time of deep reflection and holy occasion (Leviticus 23:24; Numbers 29:1-6; Nehemiah 8:2, 9-12).

God Judges

Rosh Hashanah, according to Jewish tradition, is when God looks into the hearts of people and judge their deeds and motives. It is said, that God will inscribe their names in the Book of Life or Death, and in so doing, determine who will live another year or who will die. Subsequently, Rosh Hashanah is not only a time to celebrate the Jewish New Year and the creation; it also begins what is called the "Ten Days of Awe or Penitence". Multitudinous prayers are offered, scripture reading and repentance culminates on Yom Kippur ten days after Rosh Hashanah begins. The prayers, good deeds and repentance are done being hopeful that God will look with favor upon their lives and inscribe their name in the Book of Life. To symbolize purity, some of the men will wear a white robe to the synagogue. These will be the shrouds in which the observant Jews are buried.

Rosh Hashanah, also known as the *Feast of Trumpets*, or *Yom Teruah* (the Day of the Sounding of the Shofar), *Yom ha-Din* (the Day of Judgment, and *Yom ha-Zikkaron* (the Day of Remembrance). During this holiday the "shofar", or ram's horn, is blown. The rabbis open the Ark of the Torah, the story of Abraham and the binding of Isaac is remembered.

In remembering the story of Abraham and Isaac, the religious are reminded of Isaac's rescue from death and God's mercy. The night before the holiday Jews greet one another with, *L'Shanah tovah tikatevu,* "May you be inscribed for a good year!" Apples or bread are dipped in honey to express hope and sweetness for a good next year and prayers for the peace of the world are spoken as they remember God.

Blowing the Shofar

When blown, the mystical echo of the shofar is a call to worship. Three different types of sounds pour fourth from this twisted piece of bone.

The first blast of the ram's horn is called the "Tekiah." This is one long uninterrupted blast. Second, is the "Shevarim", consisting of three blasts. Third, is the "Teruah" with nine short, pithy sounds emanating forth. Finally, the "Tekiah" is sounded once again. This is the final eerie uninterrupted piercing reverberation from this ancient horn.

There are different interpretations given as to why these various sounds and number of blasts are blown from the ram's horn. Let me give you some pertinent insight and interpretation into this magnificent tradition.

The first Tekiah is defined as a call to warning, a call to attention. Something is happening, be alert! Be watchful! Second, the Shevarim represents diversity that comes with life's experience. Some say, it encourages us to continue to move forward in our journey "forgetting those things which are behind" and pressing towards the mark of knowing God's forgiveness and mercy. It is a reminder of repentance and sorrow breaking with past sins. Third, the Teruah is closely related to the previous, as it represents weeping, pain and remorse of the penitent for their sins. Finally, the last Tekiah directs us to the final victory over sin, temptation and the flesh. It leads us to a new direction, a new path, a new beginning and a new life. (Paul referred to the final Tekiah in 1 Thessalonians 4:16, "the trump of God").

Throwing Stones

Regarding the idea of repentance and new life you will find the religious going to streams or rivers observing the water current moving down, symbolically or in reality, to the sea. Or, some of the faithful are able to go directly to the ocean depending on where they live. They recite the last verses from the book of the prophet Micah which states,

"And Thou will cast their sins into the depths of the sea"
(Micah 7:19)

Beforehand they will fill their pockets with stones, herbs or flowers, which symbolically represent their sins. Standing at the shore, the religious will cast the symbol of their sins into the water. The, idea is that the current then takes their sin into the depths of the sea never to be seen again. How comforting that thought is to the contrite soul. This is done on the first afternoon of the first day of Rosh Hashanah and is called *Tashlikh,* or Casting Off. Therefore, exercising this act, they symbolically cast their sins into the water.

So in the final analysis, Rosh Hashanah is a celebration of the anniversary of God creating the universe. God is remembered as the Supreme Judge and Sovereign over all things known and unknown and as the Living and Everlasting God. It is a time to remember that God holds our very breath in His hands and that we must give an account for our sins and trust in God's forgiveness and mercy.

Yom Kippur

Yom Kippur, or literally, Day of Atonement is the last of the Ten Days of Awe or Penitence and is the holiest day in the Jewish calendar (Leviticus 23:27-32). It is known as *"the Sabbath of Sabbaths"*. It is marked by twenty-four hours of prayer and fasting.

White is the symbol of purity and is the dominant color of Yom Kippur. The altar cloths and the Torah covers, which are maroon on the Sabbaths and blue on the festivals, are now changed to white. The story of Jonah is recited, as he was the prophet who learned that all men are God's children (according to Jewish tradition). The very pious recite responsively the entire Book of Psalms.

The Yom Kippur service is the longest in the Jewish liturgy. It begins with the chanting of the *Kol Nidre,* a prayer asking for the release from vows and promises that were not kept. Prayers continue throughout the evening and the next day. Confession of sins, or the *Viddui* is expressed. The service closes with the Neilah, or closing. It refers to the closing of the gates of heaven at the conclusion of the day. Finally, the shofar is blown and these words are exclaimed, *Leshanah habaah biyerushalayim,* "Next Year in Jerusalem!"

Christian Perspective

As with most religions, Judaism is full of beautiful ritual and symbolism. Rosh Hashanah and Yom Kippur are two of the most important holidays within Judaism. To understand a holy day of the Old Testament one must always keep in mind that ritual points to something greater that itself. Messiah is usually the presage considered.

Rosh Hashanah reminds us of new beginnings and accountability. It draws our attention to the creation of new life and meditation upon the One who created all life. Jesus said, *"I am the way, the truth, and the life: no man cometh unto the Father, but by me"* (John 14:6). John the Apostle tells us that Jesus is the source of all life and that it will be the Son of God who passes judgment, not the Father (John 1; 5:22). Also, it was Jesus who created all things and that *"He is before all things, and by him all things consist"* (John 1; Colossians 1:16,17). Plus, as mentioned earlier, the Apostle Paul, referencing the tradition of Rosh Hashanah stated, that when the trumpet (shofar, ram's horn) of God is blown the dead in Christ shall rise first (1 Thessalonians 4:16). Paul brings a clearer focus on this in 1 Corinthians 15:52 when he says, *"In a moment, in the twinkling of an eye, at the last trump: for the trumpet shall sound, and the dead shall be raised incorruptible."*

Isn't it amazing that the celebration of Rosh Hashanah was actually a foreshadow, a presage, a rehearsal for the celebration of the Messiah? This being the case, all people must examine the claims of Jesus. Is he the Messiah as he said (Matthew 27:63,64; Mark 14:61,62; John 4:25,26)? If he is the Messiah and the Creator of life and the Judge, then we must respond, either in belief or rejection. If we reject Jesus as the Messiah and Lord, we of all people will be most miserable and the eternal ramifications are very ominous (John 3:36). If we believe, then we will find peace, purpose and meaning to our lives and the eternal ramifications are very encouraging (John 3:16).

Regarding Yom Kippur, the holiest day in Judaism, we must tie together the two holidays. Rosh Hashanah is the beginning of something that will culminate at Yom Kippur.

From the first day throwing the stones in the water (*Tashlikh*) until final blowing of the shofar at the conclusion of Yom Kippur, the emphasis is on repentance and trying to appease the judgment of God.

Remember, it was on the Day of Atonement the High Priest went into the Holy of Holies to offer sacrifice on behalf of Israel. Therefore, we can understand the effort of modern day Judaism in trying to create a sobriety and reverence for such an important day. Wait a minute! The Temple is gone. The Holy of Holies is gone.

Since the Temple no longer exists it is impossible to offer blood atonement for the people. So what the rabbis have done is substitute blood atonement with *mitzvah*, a ritual obligation(s) or good deed(s).

Now we have a problem. The Scripture teaches "for it is the blood that maketh an atonement for the soul" (Leviticus 17:11). Good deeds are commendable, however, they cannot atone for the soul. Religious ritual obligation is commendable, however, rituals cannot atone for the soul.

The Scripture also teaches, "So without the shedding of blood there is not remission of sin (Hebrews 9:22). What is the answer to this problem? Yeshua (*Yeshua* is the Hebrew way to say Jesus) is the answer. He was the perfect and final sacrifice for sin (Hebrews 6-9)

Therefore, Yom Kippur and Rosh Hashanah direct us to the One who can forgive sin and bring into a right relationship with God. Jesus is God's Lamb offered for the sins of mankind. We must put our trust in Him and not depend on our own religious efforts or good deeds to gain God's approval. For eternal life is a gift received through faith and is not predicated on good deeds or religious activity (Ephesians 2:8-10). We must trust in God's mercy and grace provided for us through His Messiah, the Lord Jesus, the Lamb of God who takes away the sin of the world (John 1:29; Psalm 49:7-9; Isaiah 59:12; Leviticus 9:12; Jeremiah 31:3; Leviticus 17:11; Isaiah 53:3-10; Psalm 2:12; Proverbs 30:4; Genesis 15:6; John 11:25,26; John 14:6).

Chapter 4
Rosh Codesh

Beloved, did you know that the first day of each Jewish month is known as Rosh Chodesh? Jewish months may have 29 or 30 days. When there are 30 days, two days are celebrated: the last (30th) day of the previous month and the first day of the new month. When there are 29 days in the month, the first day of the new month is celebrated. This is the first day of the new moon.

Jewish months are based on the lunar calendar. Numbers 28:11 states, *"And in the beginnings of your months ye shall offer a burnt offering unto the Lord."* This holiday is considered a minor holiday or festival. Special blessings and psalms are recited and the reading of Numbers 28:1-15 are part of the observance.

In my opinion, the most important point is that it is a time of reflection on the past month and a pondering how one can do better in the new month.

With Rosh Chodesh in mind, may our hearts reflect on the blessings of God that came upon our lives this past year.

Let us be encouraged to serve the Lord with all our heart, soul, mind and strength in the coming year. Offer the Lord a sacrifice of praise and put into action our words of faith. May our Lord find us even more committed to Him in the days and years ahead!

Chapter 5
Tisha B' Av

Tisha *B' Av,* on the ninth of the month of Av (August), commemorates the destruction of the First and Second Temples in Jerusalem.

On the evening of the holiday, the lights are dimmed in the synagogue and the congregants sit on low benches or on the floor. Readings will be from the Book of Lamentations along with other portions of scripture that focuses on mourning and prayer. That evening a fast begins.

The ninth of Av is has a significant history for the Jews. In 135 A.D., the Bar Kochba (a false messiah) revolt against the Romans ended in defeat on the ninth of Av; One year later, on the ninth of Av, the Roman emperor Hadrian had the ruins of Jerusalem plowed under by teams of oxen and built a Roman city on its site and called it Aelia Capitolina. Jews were forbidden to enter the city upon penalty of death; in 1242 Talmudic books were burned in Paris on the ninth of Av; in 1492 Jews were driven out of Spain on the ninth of Av; in 1942 Jews were deported from the Warsaw Ghetto to the Treblinka death camp on the ninth of Av.

"This is why I weep and my eyes overflow with tears" (Lamentations 1:16).

There are many mysteries that only God knows why they happen. One mystery is Tisha B' Av.

Chapter 6
The Origin of Hanukkah

Notorious Nemesis

In 168 B.C. the Syrian emperor Antiochus came from the north and defeated Egypt. During the process of celebrating his victory he was pressured by Rom to withdraw. In his anger at this reversal, he directed his resentment towards, and made a swath through, the land of the Jews. He set out to destroy Judaism making any observance of the Jewish religion illegal. It is recorded that he would torture mothers and children publicly and then would execute them. He defiled the Temple by sacrificing a pig on the altar to the god Zeus Olympus, and then looted the Temple (Daniel 8:11-19; 11:21-35).

Mighty Mattathias

It looked as though this notorious Syrian emperor was unstoppable. However, in Modin, three miles north of Jerusalem, a Jew named Mattathias, along with his five sons began a revolt against the Syrian monarch. This small band grew in number throughout the Judean hills and within three years drove the Syrian invaders out of Jerusalem and the surrounding area. It is said, that on the 25th day of Kislev (November/December), exactly three years to the day, after its desecration, the Temple and altar were rededicated.

Miraculous Menorah

The Jews "wept" when they saw the desecration of the temple and began to restore it to a "state of ritual purity." Jewish tradition records that when the heroic Jews set about to rekindle the Perpetual Light (candle stand; seven candle menorah) there was only enough consecrated oil to last only for one day. It would take eight days to prepare ritually permitted oil. The miracle was that the oil in the menorah, which was to only last for one day, remained lit for eight days, until the special oil was procured.

Divine Dedication

Today, Jews throughout the world light candles each night during the eight-day celebration of this miracle of God. The miracle is the emphasis, not the military victory. Hanukkah, which means "Dedication", proclaims a divine miracle, not a human victory. The reason the rabbis emphasize the spiritual, although the Bible regarded some wars as just, was simply they did not allow human bloodshed to be associated with worship. David, for example, was not permitted to build the Temple because his life had been devoted to the quest of war. Hanukkah marks the rescue of Judaism, as a faith, and a way of life from annihilation.

Similar Seasons

It is interesting how Hanukkah and Christmas are similar. Both originated in the same land, by the same people, Israel and the Jews. Both are celebrated the same day in their respective months – 25th day of Kislev (November/December), and the 25th day of December. Gifts are exchanged during these holidays, special foods are prepared, candles are lit, and spiritual songs are sung. Both commemorate an historical event.

Christ Candle

The "Servant" is prominent in both holidays. The "shammash", or servant candle, which is usually in the middle of the nine-candle menorah, or on the side of the menorah, is higher than the other eight candles. The shammash is used to light the other eight candles. The rabbis teach it was the flame of faith which brought about the miracle. Its motto is found in the prophetic portion read during the festival, *"Not by might, nor by power, but by my spirit, saith the Lord of Hosts"* (Zechariah 4:6). The Hanukkah Menorah is usually placed near a window, so that all can see them from the street. This is in fulfillment of the rabbinic mandate "to publicize the miracle. According to Kabbalah (Jewish mysticism), the eight candles correspond to the name of God, which means, *"I shall be"* (Exodus 3:14).

Giving God

The shammash was given a special purpose, to light the other eight candles. On the first night, one candle is lit. The second night, two candles are lit. The third night, three candles are lit, and son on, until all eight candles are flickering with flame. The shammash, or the ninth candle, is the candle used to light the others. The flame of the shammash, or servant candle, gives of itself to create an additional flame without losing any of its own brightness. Thus man gives of his love to his fellow man without losing anything of himself. The Messiah, who came not to be ministered unto but to minister as a "servant" said in the context of Hanukkah, *"I am the light of the world; he that followeth me shall not walk in darkness, but shall have the light of life"* (John 8:12). Just as the menorah is put in the window to pierce the darkness, so it is with Jesus, who pierces the darkness of the heart and brings light.

Also, Messiah Jesus said of himself in direct connection to Hanukkah, during the "feast of dedication" (Hanukkah), *"I am the good shepherd (shammash), and the good shepherd (shammash) giveth his life for the sheep"* (John 10:11,22). Jesus chose Hanukkah as the time to reveal who He was. The evil Syrian Antiochus had a second name, "Epiphanes". His complete name and title was King Antiochus Epiphanes. Epiphanes means "God Manifest." You've guessed it, Antiochus called himself God. Jesus took this opportunity, during the celebration of Hanukkah, to proclaim that He IS God (John 10:24-42). The psalmist said there would be such a declaration. "I will declare the decree: the Lord hath said unto me, Thous art my Son; this day I have begotten thee" (Psalm 2:7). How do we know tht the psalmist was speaking of Jesus? Luke confirms this when he wrote, *"And we declare unto you glad tidings, how that the promise which was made unto the fathers, God hath fulfilled the same unto us their children, in that he hath raised up Jesus again; as it is also written in the second psalm, Thou art my Son, this day have I begotten thee" (Acts 13:32,33).*

The apostle Paul described Jesus in connection with Hanukkah in Phillippians 2:5-11. In these verses you will find the Messiah lowering himself taking on the form of a *"servant"* giving life to all who believe.

Jesus came not to be ministered unto but to minister as a "servant", "Shepherd", and "Light". The resurrection confirms who he said he was, and is.

Beloved, may we be reminded of God's love for us, humbling himself, becoming a man, taking on the form of a servant, being born in Bethlehem's cave, born of virgin to die on a cross for our redemption and forgiveness. It is truly joyous to know that Jesus is the "Light of the world"! To believe on Him is to receive the gift of eternal life.

"For God sent not his Son into the world to condemn the world; but that the world through him might be saved" (John 3:17).